CHAPBOOKS BY KOSTAS ANAGNOPOULOS

Daydream

Irritant

Various Sex Acts

MOVING BLANKET

KOSTAS ANAGNOPOULOS

UGLY DUCKLING PRESSE : BROOKLYN, NEW YORK

Some of these poems have appeared previously in the following publications: *Big Bridge*, *Court Green*, *The Hat*, *New American Writing*, *Saint Elizabeth Street*, and *Sal Mimeo*. Thanks to those editors.

Special thanks to Lisa Ano, Asari Beale, Larry Fagin, Garth Graeper, Arpine Konyalian Grenier, Carolyn Guinzio, Jesse James, Angeliki & Ted Kalamatianos, Anna Moschovakis, Shira Piven, Diane Shaw, Chris Tokar, and everyone at UDP.

LIBRARY OF CONGRESS CATALOGING-IN-PUBLICATION DATA
Anagnopoulos, Kostas.
    Moving Blanket/Kostas Anagnopoulos.
        p. cm.
    ISBN 978-1-933254-69-2 (pbk. : alk. paper)
    I. Title.
    PS3601.N35M68 2009
    811'.6--dc22
                                    2009042958

DISTRIBUTED TO THE TRADE BY
Small Press Distribution/SPD
www.spdbooks.org

AVAILABLE DIRECTLY FROM UDP & THROUGH OUR PARTNER BOOKSELLERS
Ugly Duckling Presse
The Old American Can Factory
232 Third Street, #E002
Brooklyn, NY 11215
www.uglyducklingpresse.org

PHOTO: QUEENSBORO BRIDGE CIRCA 1909, G.G. BAIN
FIRST EDITION 2010
PRINTED IN THE USA

CONTENTS

for my teachers

MOVING BLANKET

1.
No information for you today
(pointing to the book)
Not enough to bring out the atlas
It was a dreadful way to think
About the threshold and its wreath
Splashed by the same automobiles
That showed up the next morning with garlic breath
But time is cruel
Soon the clouds will come for you too
Nonetheless these poems were collated
Your expectations are in there
Shining with all their porcelain fixtures
By taking the vaccine yourself
You encourage others to come forward
Let the man with the boxes through
You don't have a Plan B
Except to work from home
Where your possessions are
They say you're better off reading the label
Which reminds me, at the crazy house
They asked us who the first president was
And they cupped our genitalia
Dull as that may seem
I told them I wouldn't leave without them
Now you're it
Stirring helps but sticking remains your biggest problem
And time is money, haven't you noticed?
The economy had better listen
Each word framed in time or scattered
Like things in a display
The way birds, trees and grass are afterthoughts

Winter moved to a new location
You expect snow and will throw warm water on it
Ledges catch it but then let it fall

2.
The snow is reflective
Clementines roll downhill
Kleenex issued to the disenfranchised many
Entering the vessel unprepared
Umbrellas gone forever
Curry in the clouds
Station after station drifted and talked
Night sky with thoughts of peaches
Save me a bite
Inching toward that rotten wisdom tooth
And don't forget these pillows are for the future
Because daylight can't keep darkness out
Make room for me under the receipts
Wouldn't you know it those same birds are hopping with suggestions now
They better keep their day jobs
Finally there's some light coming from the painting
So on special occasions you may have a taste
You're moving away from the weather
Climbing up through the olives
Riding your bike along the berm
Keeping an eye on the monument
If only through a peephole
Nothing else to add
Everything must go
Stick close to me
You're the only antennae I've got

A LESSON IN DISGUISE

The book makes you look small
In the new edition this line will be deleted
Though it's unclear why
I know we're going to lose you
To the painting across the hall
The one of Guido
The city has no memory of you
The city is made of falls
Private interest rushed in
Wiping away any trace of their scale
For the time being we won't hold a grudge
Eventually the streets will freeze over
There will be no host, no welcome wagon
Only one extraordinary item of laundry
That lost its family
That's how these things get started
Never enough childhood to go around
But plenty of common colds
Invitations to be snubbed and guided
Like any contradiction, to the parapet, and over
At least the bachelor buttons have found their friends
And there's a hint of mint in the air

The holes in my education. I am graded and come up short. How free
the birds are! They walk, too. I follow them but they are fast. The books
are small and short but slow. I study the night sky and its holes. But you
travel with a black nimbus lighting your way. Thunder interrupts our class,
leaving us dyspeptic, squabbling over nothing. We see stars without being
struck. Teacher pushes our buttons, our limbs fatten with regret. We are
after all in a land where books are left out in the rain. I'm in the lowest
percentile, having horsed around like a musical top or a page torn out. Will
the future reach me before I die?

BLINDMAN

Up the mountain on a damp night
Like a negative, darker than a park
More pink than a country

I won't be mocked
Hit on the head with green drops

In hindsight the nineteenth century
Was a cycle of interruptions
Misunderstandings devoted to understanding

Larger than life on the shelf
In the aisle we've come to rely on

Bags of clouds reflecting the climate of the times
Calling them home in the wee hours
Announcing the degrees

Cross this or that bridge
See where it gets you
Distribute the weight
Switch shoulders

Silhouettes of the Northern Song Period
Squatters in the tiger maple wardrobe

I DIDN'T CATCH EVERYTHING HE SAID

His chin moved out of the frame, showed no sign
Of our arrangement with the chisel
I gave a brief synopsis of the predicament
How the joke had spread to the galleys
How it wasn't his doing
That he was mistaken for a pump
By those who believed the hearsay
That we were witness to nothing, nothing funny
That we should have been on the interstate by then, by now
We must tell the world

INTERIOR

The moon returned to its position over the settee. What a mess
eavesdropping has gotten me into. The funeral march chased the crowd
away. Can you blame it? Everyone here is either doddering with ear
trumpets or bumping heads in the acorn shade. I amuse myself by
candlelight. Z is my pronoun. I arrived late with an excuse — I left my
tools in the grass. That's not an excuse. Okay, I've fathered hallways and
gangways, the cornice with florets, and huffed at the holy cloth. Several live
oaks have been cut down out front. Our orb of night is chipped. No open
house tonight, but the squirrels are still making the rounds with their fruit
baskets.

A piece of tape keeps our family portrait on the wall. We're dressed for a wedding. My mother is smiling, my father is smiling less and I am not smiling. This picture follows us from house to house. The great cloth appears behind us. My mother is wearing an onyx brooch. I used to rub it against the mirror, thinking it would scratch the surface. Wrong. My father has a beard. I don't have any facial hair yet. But yet has passed and we're frantic in the middle of the trade show. The paper vases and spice containers have done well. But our French book line just missed the toilet and we expected more out of our silk pillows. It's almost over anyway.

POEM

Stuffed into a snowsuit
This leg, that arm
Pumped up at the frozen pond
A dream of ice skating to Harlem
They weren't going to wait for me
Space is so difficult
Keep at it! someone shouts from the sidewalk
But dreamless sleep is best
Lest I wake up in Harlem in my shorts
Night a lonely part of day
A big sink
I switch off the light, reposition the funnel

At dawn the rain
Blank as a syndrome

I often get lost in the boys department
Mother reads to me from an index card
The poem rolls off her tongue

They laughed at my growth spurt
Kept me away with a pole
Wind, pine needles, spit
Thrown at me

Help is on the way
Many black trucks

APRIL

Like a heart in a parking lot
Or an illuminated crime in an alley
Where we got lazy with our plans for the future
And the present resumed in disbelief
We turned away from it
The clock is fidgeting
But there's plenty of headroom
In case you ever want to stop by
I've been conversing with things
Everything is a thing
Making my speeches simple and neat
Sooner or later there'll be plenty of loss
Enough to acquire its own vocabulary
But then the brickwork of the heart
Will meet you at the tollbooth
Where you'll live forever in the oncoming traffic
Otherwise not much happened this month
Some light snow
That never reached the earth
Evaporating in memory
Later returning to cover our landing

NOTHING

1.
Consisting of so many things
Repeated
They pick us
When they do they stop us
The sun in its car
Hit us like a tragedy
Rear-ended us

The nameless have fled
I won't forget them
I don't have that kind of mind

A conversation starter requiring no intelligence
Encountering many shifts in tone
Dropping and adding extraneous sounds
Drowned out by hearsay
On a tape recorder
Who knows the rules and regulations?

Words divide everything

Now isn't the time to resume our project
It remains in the vault
Let's return to a happy medium

Outside the cathedral
Crouching in the shrubbery
Too weak to take communion

You are the main noisemaker

In the Spring a timer went off
To general speechlessness
We required stillness
Pausing without a pause
Delighting in stalling
Now at the end of our walk

Our bliss was imperfect
The foul air became crisp
And bright lights cast by the squid boats
Played across our expectant faces
As we traveled to all the attractive ports
I love the marquee
Their Transient Measures
I can't wait to understand it
Look but don't touch
Listen
The words say one thing but mean another

The moving faces
Pass slowly along the wall
A visual lullaby
Requiring some skill to observe
Not realizing how slow they move
I fill out the questionnaire

That design is worth remembering
I shifted for a better view
But I'll never remember time passing
It's too much!
Even with all the earmarks in the world to guide me
The decorations paralyzed me

Marzipan on every doorstep
In every window display
Rally for the Festival of Lights
I must ingest it all!

2.
The vines climb little by little
It's only Tuesday
Bricks repeat
People are absent
Working on their schemes
To pass the time
Socks hung out to dry
The old rack
If you're sniffling why not blow your nose
The magic of pragmatism
Turn the air on before turning it off
There will be other times, other territories
Things no one sees or remembers
A wall is in their way
It gives them lip
It's in a world without hinges
Slamming shut
On freaks with crumbs
Strings
Skipped a beat
And clap
As the dust settles

3.

Under my bed I found...zilch

Everything ended up where it should be

I looked some more

Under the mattress

Behind the headboard

Moving parallel to the fire

That was spreading

An orange sky

Tremendous heat

People in bubbles

Released in a frenzy

Incubators

They experience loss for the first time

Open yourself up to it

Open up

You'll see

4.

Finish what you started

But keep the whole world for yourself

In lieu of weeds

Rubble on the overpass

Each unfinished thought

Drizzle

Your limited vocabulary

Slurred

Air touches you

APPEARANCE ALONE

Once upon a time is reminiscent of your eyes
Appearing in a poem by accident
Or in a fairy tale told on a rainy day
I mistook the rain for a description of your sad eyes
And now you must stop using the word *once*
When you look out the window
Something will look back at you
But only once
All is contingent on pointlessness
Windswept through the penny arcade
Giving the appearance of dead time
The past is not healing as quickly as you'd like
Within is an abstraction of the way out
Logical places exist in illogical books
But reality can't be miniaturized as a mental object
Or a marker for reflection
No logic needed, dead to the world
Blinking light at the end of the tunnel
Don't get rust on your lens
Nor does public opinion matter
It's best to have less than others
This has been said before, I know
Propaganda isn't what you think
In a thinking poem, which this is not
It's a conversation I'm having with you
The house is empty now
Fragile as eyes

MAGPIE

The earth is not our friend
That was a false impression
We can't wait for inspiration, nor do we wish to
Hang around where hormones are raging
Repellents have been suspended
I've seen carpets swallow people whole
I arrived at the filter via the puddle
Where I twisted a dial
Without getting clobbered by some federation
A depression appeared in the glass
I'd forgotten our signal
The pursuit ran this way
The charitable arm that dampened
The missing post on its way out
We sat quietly while the sun spun
The gist of it
It caused flooding and another day of questioning
Then we were back to weed whacking
The grass was groomed, the bushes blurred
Losing sight of the slope in the fog
However much it glowered on the horizon
I've become a regular
In a minute I'll be washed ashore
Not pinned up in the portrait gallery
Dog factories have been springing up everywhere
I was about to be married off
When my eyeballs opened
And the critics came out to eat walnuts
They did little or nothing for my poems
I hid in the wardrobe from family and friends

Then the baby came along
The bundle drenched on the stoop
And a new batch of documents had been issued
In the hot spray, epitomizing the loss of baby
Insiders were magnetized by the window
Filled with variants
It's going to be a wet Friday they said
The city was room temperature
The teams, the bridges catalogued
All weeds yanked and catalogued
In the after-life where they end up anyway
The man in orange gone to direct the festivities
In the branches, telling the birds, poor things, where to get off
They haven't listened to him thus far
Why should they now?
Stop stirring
Be silent but not passive, says an important man
Information is available at the booth
The passwords are *you* and *beans*
We don't live by those words anymore
Things fall apart
Yes, and people, too
The imprint of wicker on their backs
What does the lawn have that I don't have?
Why are there receipts in the weeds?
How come I feel suffocated by umbrellas?
You'll never know
What life would be like with more negative space
As in the French bon *(bon)*
Used to indicate that the preceding vowel is nasalized
As if that was what held you back
The new rules will take effect at midnight
The idea of nothing connecting

If you like we can put a medicinal tree in your window
You won't even know it
The dollar keeps falling, falling on our heads
For months the family tried to get their son back
From the other place, one in which
I gallop because I'm on fire
A trigger happy puffball
Rarely do I walk
I can't remember ever being on a path
Life is even shorter in these parts
Middleburg. Hang a left
At the Acropolis
Comb snarls out of your ears
I can't live with this banging
I'll let go now, move to the bottom of the hill
Please don't follow me
The blue has sunk us for good
Heavy with questions
Heavier than answers
Who knew the clouds were full of water
And behind them the birds were coming unglued?
In the long run much depends on our understanding of
How the pool works
Openings keep closing
On an optimistic note, the biopsy revealed nothing
Nothing they could *see* anyway
Evening is a good time for tunnel glazing
The moles had a pleasant conversation in the tunnel
The tunnel takes my breath away
Ultimately I understand the outcome of my circumstance in the bedroom
Forecasters study the comets by sniffing
The result can be a dangerous vacuum
Best to stay out of it

Being comatose on the job makes you an easy target

Projections come closer to reality

In fact, here they are now

The tea stains

The sub-committee never made it to the floor

Tennessee's problems run deeper than ours

Hazy hot and humid today

One year from now we'll be moved to a gated community

Our bolts in the rain under a canopy of brights

Moscow is lit with new bearded folk

Other life has surfaced by accident

We set aside our cons

We figured out that much by ourselves

A little bird told me to lay low

It was a false bell

Next time I'll be your sewer

I'll release your dilemma into the river

For they have put us in our place for good

Why all the extra forsythia bushes?

INVISIBLE BOY

Adding to the heap of misshapen conventions, I was defrocked. I knelt to kiss the ring. Eventually, I'll be forgotten by my handsome peers, will proceed along a solitary path, always eating alone. It's as though they never knew daylight and were unable to spot me. I would need to weigh the matter, perhaps write a petition to dead relatives. A father drives away forever. On the other hand, we should learn to support ourselves, ask questions and promote via satellite the holes from which we grow. Suddenly it hits me — darkness is seconds away. Don't argue.

WHAT HE DOESN'T KNOW

might extinguish him. He falls to the floor. He can't start over. Yes he can, folded, spindled, it's his turn — with limitations. Who goes there? It's only me. Yeah, that's what he told his father in the delivery room when they held him up to the big window, the cue for his new personality. Need any help? No, I can manage. Show me your lifeline. It's blank, I don't want it. Don't fuck it up. Let's hope not. You look a little puffy and blue from your ride. I'm sorry, do I know you? I'm Paul. Did you come with those guys? We have some things in common, blasting our music, joining in on the chorus. The body is a small one but long in parts. What do you feel when you can't speak? I feel lopsided, my grammar is off. My real father is a sailor. He'll put you on the right boat, make your passage worth it. You need a little empathy. I'm sure we can find a book on that topic.

ESCORTED BY THE SUN

The cloud took the cure. What does it matter, you ask. Well let me tell you
about the silver lining. Your brain is ceramic so you can't see. The pane, too,
is full of depressions, making the branches look gold. Builders feature it. I
reach back and feel your stubble in my palm. The kitchen will flood, you'll
see. Our time together will have passed. More people will be born. We'll
be plugging away at the office. Our shaky footing will need helping hands.
But no one comes forward, reaches out. The entire neighborhood is sound
asleep. Everything shakes, radiates.

WAKING DREAM

With our usual ceremonial airs we walk into a Radio Shack to buy a plug.
The salesman shouts at an old woman, where would you be without our
cords! I love the robot — Robbie is it? I let them sleep for another fifteen
minutes, then I blow a little horn and check the aerial photos. We're
shrinking. What concrete measures should we be taking? Look at the
bottom, I've come all undone. Is there a chance you might return me?
But there is no outlet for us. Take a number. I have some of your personal
smoke in my lungs, let me know when you'd like it back. Hours later I lower
myself onto the sidewalk, hands first. It turns out we've been on Avenue of
the Americas all along. They've let these churches alone, why not us?

I wheel myself down the street. Where would I be without my wheels? In hell, no doubt. I'm ready to plow into all the surprises heading my way. While rain lathers up the gutter, critics talk about maintaining appearances. I've bumped my noggin, sprained my ankle, slammed my fingers in doors, all while working my imagination. In this way, danger makes sense. No teacher can equip us with new limbs. We feel the pain only if it's on paper. If these pants don't fit, my mother can always alter them. They might as well be painted on.

POEM

My mother's needle put me through school
If my mother were a fruit
She'd be a fig
And I her little blood orange
I am sealed in this fruit world
I don't even have a proper name
Nonetheless a routine
My window is a warped one

CLOSED TODAY

Come back tomorrow
Milling around in the anteroom
Those potholes were extra bumpy
A crutch at the bottom of the pond
Ducks moved around
Life was good when they were wet
Then they let the green one back in
A mosaic flashback
Do you see it?
Is it?
The silent one goes away
The light is perfumed with hyacinth
They're sawing out back
Preserving the dust
But they're wavering
A punch in the arm and they're down
Never mind that I sped over here without a helmet
Passing through ick in good faith
Blanketed by those digits you know so well

PASTORAL MINIATURE

That's all I need
Great things are small
The domestic, the odd-sized paper
Octagonal tiles in the hallway
Make me behave hermaphroditically
Pulled apart
Yet in a state of grace
Where you travel, whether or not you're on time
Doesn't count
When you put small on a pedestal — a little pedestal
Laundry and laurel are separated by laureate
Shake off the leaves
Hogans and igloos, soup and sandwiches
Always expected on a coat of arms
On foot in the weeds the aesthete in hoop skirt cries out
At the mere mention of alabaster
The thought doesn't count
You prevail
There are no details
You are made of them
Pick your own berries
At least until it snows
But remember the petroglyph
Its finicky composition, a tour of sorts, back to nature
Brush off the dust, come up with your own little itinerary
Unpeel labels that shouldn't have stuck
These too have entered your bloodstream

WALNUT

I was hoping for a nice finish

But ended up with a fat lip

Times are tough

Just a trim, thanks

My street is called Near Road, I thought you'd like to know

And I don't want to move into the past as quickly as the rest

I'm fine right here

The little rascals play in the patchwork field

With their bayonets

They size me up

Pointing their fat fingers

When I wake up

A fine spray is tickling my chin

We were too close together

So I put up a panel

I'm happy when I'm on my own

I don't drive so I don't get around much

I listen to the ice shift in the eaves

The heat gurgle

The fridge spasm

Not by choice

I'm waiting for the Vikings

To swing by and pick me up

ON IMPULSE

I love double features
There's no sense of real time
I like dead flowers too
An aspect of New York you forget
What I once knew may never come up again
Etherealize when I'm moving things around
Sloppy
In mother's garage I was
Still am, a prisoner
Would like nothing better than to be turned into a woman
In one of those movies
Over an urban hedge
I'd be alone
But with what fire!
A new kind of nun
Coarse as salt
With my starched coif
Melancholic as concrete
Sucking on cloves
Lugging my valise across big anterooms
Spitting thoughtfully without warning
Reading
Reading what?
It doesn't matter, short stories
Smoking of course
Looking around

for L.A.

MUSICAL NUMBER

"The sea around us"
Thus spake the pig to the farmer who had interned with the cow
And again dissonance found a new way to engage the improbable gash
Made by a large horn
Perhaps a sarrusophone
Or reasonable interference within the dainty home
Tonight is darker than the rest, everyone agrees
Senses mix and evaporate
There's no distribution of the above
The place of arts and letters in a kingdom hard pressed
Yet work is issued in part only
Securing the plural in each of us
An electric ray has hit town
Not requiring an entrée
Once outside your mental hutch
You resemble the nuthatch
Hot in its upside down precision
Blurry lines all over the island
Leaning on the white keys
All is redolent of strict formation
For what is not tied down floats away

You can always put another mirror there, at least until the lights come back on. With mirror there, outside comes in, all one family, though the trees framed in gold say something different about history. I don't care. I'd rather study the wallpaper with its pattern of tormented tulips or admire pen flourishes of recent officials. I don't know the meaning of sitting still. All this talk of blinking lights is likely to crop up somewhere in a speech. You just don't want it there. Momentum tries hard enough to build on its own. I reiterate: I would like the mirror there, no lights, just trees, and if possible let them be orange because what's better than orange this time of year? Lock the door behind you, Droopy wants to see me. I'd invite him in if it weren't for his organ. All is damp. I'm getting hoarse. In a perfect world we wouldn't have throats. Here's the doctor. He's old, practically a ruin, but his coconut lozenges really hit the spot.

OLD NEWS

Mr. Hope died today at 100
I grip the pole and squeeze my eyes shut
Weak hearts run in my family
Leg problems too
My grandmother walked for miles every day, now she's paralyzed
She had a pretty front yard
The Hudson makes my eyes itch
An uncle of mine came to America, didn't like it, and threw his tie
      into a canal

TWO PEOPLE

One determined and one not
The dead duck at their feet
Where one sweeps up
And one collects it
Enough already with the collections
Where am I in all this?
You can't take it with you
I was living under a bridge of folding chairs
I never called for anything
No medicines
Though I worried about mildew
Stretched my lungs
Like the huge accordions of long ago
Rebutting hearsay took a lot out of me
I was flat on my back
Listening with the wrong ear
For the right sign
The leaves kept turning
Hanging around for their birthdays
But that's all
Sunlight hurts, not its brightness
But the things in the room are a momentary wash
And they think
Do we need this
Not this

Once we were in a moving vehicle the clouds sat still. I don't mean to imply anything like sadness. A turn of the page was payback for the runaway marigolds. That is, what you see on paper are mere pop-ups compared to live things — a desire to move on after a moment of regret. It's possible the plates shifted underfoot. That's why we were flung across the room.

REPORTER

Pedaling through the smoking ruins
Flowering for nostalgia's sake
I knew you superficially
The identical background, columns arranged by height
The collapse of a rock pile
I sit on our bench again
Things are happening around me
A body is fished out of the East River
The sun peeks through cracks in the limestone
A face takes a wrong turn
Buried in a man's shoulder
Yes the pages are turning for now
Keeping up with what never seems to happen
And never will

THANKS FOR REMINDING ME

You didn't make a sound when you hung the picture
At noon in the nettle patch
Which got carpeted over in the excitement
I owe you one
But for now goodbye
I'll have the whole flat to myself
The cow in the empty lot a memento
Of all my homes in the city
And on the range
Ignore the touchstone
It tells you nothing
And the socks tied in a knot like a daffodil on the windowsill
The wind will get it
I did what I was told, followed my nose
Through patterns that do and don't repeat
Along Northern Boulevard

TRAVELER

Speakers in my ears
They carry me away
They read me like a thermometer
I hand them my card
Telling them to call before it's too late
One must work fast in this business
Pilgrims rest on their pilgrimage to me
They cross a foggy bridge
Holding tight to the icy railing
They've got some pretty good readymade comebacks
Short sentences full of useful advice
Tonight we'll take a different route to the mini-mall
Where there's a museum of the insides
Don't go on about how bad it is
Or how good
Keep it short
And don't get bogged down in the consequences
Sequences are more than enough

Branches hug me
Scratch my back
Knock at my knees
The stone is my friend
Life is short
Night is the illusion of it
It's no fun when the porch light goes on
Here are my clothes
They don't fold with me in them
I'll have more to dish out later
If you can take it
Come again

SUMMER BEFORE LAST

I was lost in the mountains with Joe
The whole town was looking for us
When they found us they slapped our faces good
The house at the side of the road
Still stands today, our childhood home
With many broken chairs and crooked beds
We're grateful they found us but enough already
Grandmother rolls up her sleeves
Grabs her rolling pin
And advances menacingly
All of a sudden we're running down the hill
Grandma in hot pursuit
The village is a mud village
Only one person lives there in the rainy season
Wagadu
Then everything shifted
We were back home again (or so they said)
Counting fruitcakes, a job with benefits nonetheless
It's all personal
For example, I have pictures of you misusing your stuffing
Overall we can at least say that we're well fed
We exchange warm words
Fill our hats with water
A reminder that we're hot
And cold when we finally do get wet

MAY

I try to catch the ball
The one painted with stars
A homely thing
Out past its curfew
Chucked it at the plastic dish
Night was frozen in position long enough
Drinking a tea of lights, not actual tea
From this end, May is the way to further development
A glass orb arrives
At the door of our branch
Whom should we thank?
I close my beautiful window
To what I already miss
Daily repair of other words
This acknowledgement
A mark among many marks
Made over again
Since the books can't remember
I'll point them out for you
If it weren't for this month
Where would all the revolutions go?

TODAY

My classmates are drowsy
I don't bring it to teacher's attention
Surely they'll zero in on the prize
And I'll give way to the big girl
Not a bad thing to do
It's about who can dig deepest fastest
Yet we all seem to be equally unqualified
Even the glue has dried in the shape of a question mark
What I need is a calendar to point
To where I'll be while the dogwood festival goes on without me
I can't exactly leak it to the local press
Because they'll just have a change of heart
And plug in the pink lights
It's going to be a long night
Tomorrow will be even longer
So I'll give it a pass
Before this existence is comprised of everything
Though that wouldn't be a first

ELEVEN POEMS

1.

The sun on my face and chest
Won't give or budge
I relocate to the back porch
My eyes shine like bowls
Their glazes
Contain all of me

2.

Find time to sit
In the black Hitchcock chair
I'm afraid I'll break it
I cock my head to speak
I'm never lonely
This table does some good
The windows help
It's why we moved here
I always say I can write anywhere
That's not true
I need to be in this place
Its pre-war details
I should listen to myself but I don't

3.

Hide from the others
Avoid instruction
The mailbox is a friend
Inhaling bits of life
Relatives snore
Duck them as well
I am a balloon or a lesson
ABCDEFGHIJKLMNOPOULOS
I pop
Bach is on the box

4.

I'm not as quick as you
I'm the type who would pause at the fountain
I am a pantry man
One who finds pleasure in flour
Leaflets and jars of tokens
I'm closed like an open book
Nobody sees my cold feet

5.

I love beginnings, and much later
Tattered as a mutt's ear
To egg on an ending
It's why I never leave the apartment
Never sign up
With a broken arm
What is the sum
Think of a good epitaph

6.

Once they were captured near the bolster pillows
The mild ones
Done with tumblers for the season
And you need to be told off
Casually, but then day breaks
Into its colors, I'm hooked
Knocked around, jimmied with a flower
And I fall in with that mute bunch
Flocking to an area
Lock the door behind you

7.

How did you get so mistranslated, folded into the eggs
Whisked away to the sinkhole
Scraping off your remaining paint
Why not slip into something
More compatible with your dogma
Close the book for now
Give it to me, come on
I look at my feet
And run

8.

On the flipside
I spill my sack, all its contents
Are there any options?
The climate wasn't good for walking
I was taken out behind the barn
Where they erased my smirk
Allowed my nose to hit their clubs
It's business, they shrugged
Waving to their ovine friends
Recordings of my bleats
Have reached the other shore
In case you didn't catch it live

9.

I was the first in my family
To come through without a scratch
America a blank slate
Place to rest my head
Slip off my boots, encore
Tell me you don't see me with your eyes

10.

On foot I maintain a certain speed
Gradually become invisible
To understand me you must lose me
Just as I need to leave the party
In order to enjoy it

11.

Last time I checked in here
I pinched myself
I couldn't believe I was supported
But I was
But not by what I thought

THOUGHT BALLOON

Scenes from life glued on a bottle
We're coming closer to war
I want peace
So I walk to work and man the phones
A hundred years ago
I would be gutting fish for a living
But now I can see that you like me
Regardless of the repercussions
I remember writing to my father
I love you *dead* — instead of *dad*
Mother reminds me that I killed him
By being fey
But I digress
My time here isn't lost
I'm not just a volunteer
Or a victim of your medium
Where is the social circle I was promised
And why isn't my concerto on the charts?

PRAYER

Piety isn't something I'd recommend
Unless you can break the tedium of it
With sneezes
In Stereophonic Sound
The people a few pews away
Appear to be speaking a foreign language
That is English
But with words missing
Showing a row of teeth
Or counting on their fingers
Or moving in the pattern of a bat
You'd like to think their open-ended nature is childlike
That they can't hold off
And you will have changed your mind often
Looking for some semblance of a tract
Which isn't
What you need to read here now

POEM

Feed the pigeons
Wait! don't feed them
Wake her for the eclipse
Rosy sky, dark earth, steps ahead
The eyes of the children are nets
A relief near a garden, unused to reflecting
The madonna of plainness and regret
Overwhelming the heart with sorrow
Paste it on the kiosk and run

for Olympia

PINK TUB

Grandmother was a child and an animal. She listened to the priest who was part gypsy, part goat, atop a plastic tub knocked over by speedy kittens who had just given birth to kittens of their own. That was grandmother. Cars would kill all those kittens one day. I brought milk to begin the feeding. She has never been to sea. The tub serves as a boat, holds clothespins. She washes in it. A pink thing of global proportions gone unnoticed, now back in the spotlight, transparent yet more present than a mountain, scuffed on its underside.

for Ginna Triplett

FINAL PERFORMANCE

The researchers curled up together. The stage became a bed and breakfast
of sorts, actors occasionally missed their marks but what of it? A certain
owl would paper the auditorium. Trees lose their footing on the quad. We
won't be going back to school. That's final. Our grace period is long gone.
Let's choose a bright smiling color for the halls, one with more potential
to hide the streaks. What was it that got us into so much trouble? Streaks
were instrumental in the board's decision about whether or not to keep
us on. Easy does it, men, face forward but don't fade out. Our old cowhand
was crabby this morning, he wouldn't budge from the range. Yet there are
moments that haven't flagged since they were predicated. Even a mention
of one can bring down the house.

SPRING

Poor thing keeps dry
With its tail over its head
Everything else is drenched
Dark in its dampness, darker in the light
When we flip the switch
Everything outside goes black
Not open to eyes
My thoughts tiptoe to me
Fabric thoughts
Each containing a pinch of salt
Like that soup of yours
Leaves confound the trees
I go behind them
Tree is my dressing room
Wind tells me who lives here
Breath, the kind that comes up
In conversation, is always underfoot
With its reminder
That we're in such crummy condition
All along we've used our beaks for survival
Paper bags filled with country air
We fear we'll lose them too
Shoes laced electrically
Walking by that pitiful memorial
We seldom look at
And the street is as empty as the grammar school auditorium
That's odd, considering what's being offered

You try to think like the tree, on your head because you're in reverse. I've added some poor opinions of you to the soup. Stir and serve. There's no logic to the streets, poets put them in order, shading the doors with soft lead. We've had to buff our nails, they were bound to hurt someone. How did this melancholic baggage arrive? We took in a matinee of boiled oats with the nuns from across the courtyard. Bubbles have risen to the plaster flora in the rectory. The territory is covered but you're still paraphrasing without a map, silent as always, primping the night away. To the left, a lectern. Behind it, a lemon, headed toward the parishioners. Let's avoid him. Race you to the monkey bars.

OPEN LETTER

Thank you
I've been advised that there's nothing to do but
Dry up and blow away
That never happened
Otherwise negotiating these disappointments takes a lot out of one
Carry the one
I've tried faking drowsiness, falling down, an obvious ruse
Don't forget I've lived outside myself for some time now
Though I haven't gone very far
Growing comfortable with blank stares
Coordinates of my location follow
Hear those motors?
We're up in the air
And away we go

THE LOST BOY

Logic took me somewhere else
Then I returned to the crooked place
Where you live
I believe for a good reason
So let's pick up where we left off
Found out the hard way
I fell out of the sling
And then that tremendous heat on the deck
Made me what I am today
In spite of my limited wardrobe
I was dragged down by carbohydrates
It'd be nice to return to the moon debris
But rummaging around up there isn't an option now
The department started a fire
I have no objective
Only an array of pins in a map
We're close to agreement
Coming from the perspective of never having been here
Even by accident
Here is a plank
Ask for different answers
I wouldn't wish those briquettes on anybody
There are non-violent ways to approach the struggle
System of vines
I stay behind my shutters
Please don't question my rationale
Especially when the drips have already dropped
Waves have been regarded
We would have received them earlier
If it hadn't been for the tropical depression
You can find me eating grapes in the planetarium
It's dark in here

We're staying overnight
I don't have anything better going for me
And if I don't care where I am
I'm not lost

THE SAD TRUTH

I don't recall your name or face
Someone else's memory indicated a paragon
A pearl circling you, insisting it's you
Tall as a pool or a horse's neck
Don't bother to listen, the music is all wrong
Still it's better to be seated up front
In case someone falls, jumps or is pushed
From the second balcony
It's happened before
Maybe not here but somewhere
But don't sweat the details
What good would it do?
The island is dangerous enough as it is
Flatness depends on you
To follow your nose on solid ground
Requiring a certain la-di-da
When you don't know the all-encompassing thing
Hang onto me
I'm like a walking stick
It's new to me too
I admit it on the very first page
Chuck it into the fire
Before it starts to play again
We'll count on your humming
So it's settled
Time goes by and everyone is alone
Ordinarily we wouldn't have chosen it for ourselves
But here we are

POEM

This is a perfect world
With its young priests and schools of marine life
Tossing their greetings aloft like a pizza
Landing in whiteness
Wringing out their bathing suits
In the teasing air
I'll wait here until all these particles are absorbed
By their prisms, aligning themselves with my morning routine
And all goes blank as a cannon
Stuffed with confusing petitions
Apparently I've done more harm than good
To the cracked specimens
But I'm the one with the adhesive, couldn't ask for a better spot
Up here on the plateau
A boy next to me points to a ball
I ask him if he wants it
His father who is in a wheelchair
Signs to the boy
Who responds by shaking his head
The ball is deflated

TONIGHT

The eclipse is blushing
It knows what's in store for it tonight
Darkness is well-stocked with pink
Pink marble, pink skin, pink pig
The cosmos in the rain
Droplets manage to get inside
Despite our great electric buttresses
And here's mother with a message on a string
It's only an aside to top off your well-rounded view
Of a maternal relationship coming to an end
The premier flywheel for the mechanism of the universe
Mumbling in the middle of all this black activity
To recap, the back entrances are exits
The child looks up
The mother looks down
She points to the moon
For the rest of the evening the child walks
On the mother's dress, a magic carpet
He feels squeezed between the feature and the specialty
His dream is to be locked in a pencil case all night
He doesn't register detail yet
And I have begun to lie

DOME

Working overtime for people we never see
On top of that there's more snow
More shoveling for us and our neighbors
But you can't bicker with the weather
When it has you by the ears
In a re-enactment of the wash cycle
With a buffer off to one side
It's an eyesore, I know
Try not to fight it
We have to do our time
The envelopes are empty, stacks of them
Replacing the walls
You pop out of your cubicle, tear at your wrapper
You're only human, though not in so many words
A plus at this point, you know it from practice
Their magic is to appear then run away
The dome contains all that concerns us
The bagpipes got it wrong
Men lost their breath on the field that day
Parading bumper to bumper through the metropolitan area
As though they mandated it
We sure didn't
A shroud in a darkening chamber
Falls apart, worn out
We don't have anywhere to go
Somewhere with nice quiet people

ON THAT NOTE

Sharing (printed) stories that common sense tells us are lies. Break
all the eggs, whisk them in a petrified bucket that's likely to pop up
in a museum sooner or later. We're being held by the dispatcher.
I'm reminded of what I have to do before I go. The trick to capturing
milkweed. I've learned everything by rote, consider myself part
ventriloquist, part immigrant. I am also a weight, placed in a refrigerator,
happy to have somewhere to be during the delay. I've been naturalized,
that's apparent, but let's keep it strictly *entre nous*.

AUBADE

A quiet epic
Rubbing the heels of the garbage
A jolt of lime zest
Pressing forward to noon
The shield for today, keep it up
Because there were so many things wrong with yesterday
So many things right
Things to do or make
A grayness once we passed the sprockets
And they cut off our cuffs
Morning as a means to an end
Of earth's melancholy, a splash
Where thoughts are blessed
The poor mind comes and goes
Among these which are not its
I am happy to have met the bird
Eyes so large and orange
The world can't see life, can't see
The period ending
Hope is buzzed in
She's hung a sweater out to dry
Over the railing
Morning is an awning
We dare not put up
Afraid we might spoil
Without the sun's help

for Lauri Faggioni

CLOGGED SINK

Night is fading
Day is nigh
Cars start up
A man walks out the door
And through another door
A headache persists
A squirrel is eating at the sill
Lead paint will take care of him
But the next day he brings a friend
Good friend
They say it's all good
Chinese music is playing at this time
He'd sell his soul to get more sleep
I am he
The stovetop glows
Since today is still yesterday, God knows what's to become of us
In the vestibule where I recline
Antibodies reckon with me
While the antibody I built a personal relationship with
Breaks down
Extend your paw

The archer comes up for air, aiming at latecomers. He's already applied for the position of 19th century fossilist. You can imagine the strain. They'll create a quilt for him of patches suggesting rooms. I've pointed it out once before when I broke the fleur-de-lis over his curly head. The tree is a cloud. Cupid withdraws. Sooner or later that dial is going to fall on someone. Then it's goodbye thermos. Forget your dreams of the happy life. Black clouds will land here to block the future. Cherubic limbs will be airborne popcorn. Leave at once for the brambles.

What a nice voice. The walls are thick but I hear her singing. Now she's informing the police. Ignore what you've learned. Ignore me too. The days are not passing, are stuck here, winter astringent. Thank god for that twill over her face. Brightness begins. Many people were "compiled." Sooner or later they'll recognize each other. I'm on break. They're cutting down more sequoias. Take one.

POEM

Thrown cold into the story
Your strong back

Having screened your thoughts behind the beaded curtain of the rain
All is parallel

Until you're sent to the corner to do as you wish
Useless as those groins in the ceiling

Otherwise they say it's jail
Need I remind you cash is best?

These measures are no longer for your benefit
But they do take a little pressure off the courts

MEXICAN RESTAURANT

It's not meant to be but is
Where everyone eats and no one speaks
Until the unnamed storm catches up with them
Blows them out of the joint
A snaking cord
Let out of the bag
No time to measure its end
Fed back into the least expected artery
Pondering, turning away, I overheard it
Buried in the covers
Not many seats left
Not the way they usually went
Watch out for thorns because that body is abnormal
So they returned it to the freezer
You were going to finish off the last serif
As though the alphabet were telling you some blocked secret
Put it back the big voice said
I don't believe in vacuums
Lattice of vines
Blocked light
Green candy on the floor
How long before someone steps on it?
Why are they stuck here?
A better life, I guess
Don't go there

Let this mural be a vast one, a showplace where muscular bodies leap from pad to transparent pad. Let their pajamas appear with thumbnail moons to remind us how minuscule we are. You can't fit everything into the grid. These plaques have a lifespan too. In the end they'll be the only real estate left. Or else some poor old tree stump. Drumbeats carry us down the street. We'll lose them eventually. Keep your head up. The dancers need something to focus on, our bonnets for instance. I play down among the plastics. Don't remind me that there's more plastic than plankton in the sea. It's all uphill and who wants that? I could use an extra hand, especially with trillions of these widgets to rearrange. Do you know what language I speak? I speak *show me*.

PLACE STAMP HERE

Shaking it makes them appear
Glowing on the periphery
Proving only that space is occupied at all points
Do I care?
Of course
I'll glow if it's the last thing I do
The yard is taking a real beating
People throw miscellaneous crap everywhere
As though it all ends with us
But it doesn't
No clouds come around
We must wait to be seeded for the silence to break
And that alone isn't enough for an address
Speaking clearly and distinctly
Yet with parched throats
Timing is everything when you are the issue
I climb over the rocks and onto the boat
With all the other poets

LOUISIANA

They are not in the business of noticing
But today they looked my way and guess what
They noticed
So look my way
Let me tell you a story about the ties that bind
All claims must be made within five days
Yet I have a desire for a clean slate
I'm always starting over
Compensating for my fuck-ups
Listing them on the big board
Don't ask for more
We're moving fast, falling behind
Under the bleachers by Seymour Butts
It's all landfill, this life
With perches for the pelicans

POEM WITHOUT PORTFOLIO

Waiting around for ideas I had late last night
To show up this morning
Measuring the distance between reason and impulse (six inches)
Here's my to-do list
I haven't the heart to cross anything off
Especially the things I don't do
Tomorrow will be here soon enough
That's a joke, son
Sometimes jokes can be serious
And brightness because it awakens you
Even small doses of it
Does it do it for you?
No? Well look around
We might as well be living in a culvert
That green pole is holding everything up
Big clearance sale
Under the big top
With camp beds for paying customers to stretch out on
All except you
You're an ascetic not a consumer
You deny life's little pleasures
They don't do it for you, not a one
Because you think there's more to life, for pete's sake
Stop it
Come back to me, love me
Tell me what you really think of us
Perhaps mother will guide you down the aisle
Oh yeah, that's right, she can't

The leaves are beginning to fall and there are bad dreams. Went to bed hungry, woke up full. Soon all will be yellow, then gone. I haven't applied myself, rode in a deflated car, was robbed of my assets. The perps lived in a quiet district. I recall what was taken in some detail. My cat is by my side. It is an interesting time. But I couldn't take another robbery. No break in my mind. Too late to catch sight of the bird, only a tip of her wing.

BETTER UP CLOSE

Illustrate it for me
It could be a problem you're facing
There's still sound in us

The projectionist sheds light on a boulder
An image we took
Like a powder

Some things shouldn't be forgiven
The uses of a level
What was mentioned in passing

Turn back to the wake, what a cold heart
Large with light-engorging darkness
This happy lamp you are

COLOPHON

TYPE ⦙ PMN CAECILIA, VAG ROUNDED

PAPER ⦙ NATURE'S BOOK PARTIALLY RECYCLED

GRAPHICS ⦙ AESTHETIC MOVEMENT, NY

Printed by Thomson-Shore
in an edition of 700 paperback and 200 clothbound.

75 clothbound copies are signed and numbered by the author
and are packaged with a letterpress broadside.